BECOME AN AVIATION PRO

Flight Training, Aircraft Care & More

Margo Gates

Abdo & Daughters
MIDDLE GRADE NONFICTION
An imprint of Abdo Publishing
abdobooks.com

ABDOBOOKS.COM

Published by Abdo Publishing, a division of ABDO, PO Box 398166, Minneapolis, Minnesota 55439.

Printed in the United States of America, North Mankato, Minnesota
102024
012025

Design: Denise Hamernik, Mighty Media, Inc.
Production: Mighty Media, Inc.
Editor: Katherine Chu

Cover Photographs: Adobe Stock (airplane, control tower, gauge, pilot's hat, navigation tablet); Shutterstock Images (belt loader, cockpit background, hand tools, headset, mirror, seatbelt, vest and wand)

Interior Photographs: Adobe Stock, pp. 3, 11 (top right), 12 (top left, bottom left), 13 (bottom), 14 (top right, bottom), 15 (top left, bottom left), 48–49 (background), 57, 61 (top); George Grantham Bain Collection/Wikimedia Commons, p. 8; Glenn Research Center/Wikimedia Commons, p. 6 (bottom); Kiefer/Wikimedia Commons, p. 9 (top); Mighty Media, Inc. (project photos), pp. 50, 51; Shutterstock Images, pp. 4, 5 (all), 10 (all), 10–11, 11 (top left), 12 (top right, bottom right), 13 (top left, top right), 14 (top left), 15 (top right, bottom right), 16, 17 (all), 18, 19 (all), 20, 21, 22, 23 (all), 24 (all), 25 (all), 26 (all), 27 (all), 28, 29, 30, 31 (all), 32, 33, 34 (all), 35, 36 (all), 37, 38 (all), 39 (all), 40, 41 (all), 42 (all), 43 (all), 44 (all), 44–45 (background), 46 (all), 46–47 (background), 48 (left, right), 50–51 (background), 52, 53, 54, 56, 58, 59 (all), 60, 61 (bottom); Smith Archive/Alamy Photo, p. 7; Syced/Wikimedia Commons, p. 11 (bottom); US Department of the Treasury/Flickr, p. 9 (bottom); Wikimedia Commons, p. 6 (top); ZUMA Press, Inc./Alamy Photo, p. 55

Design Elements: Adobe Stock (airplane texture, metal plates texture, Polaroid frame, sky texture, sticky notes, tacks)

Library of Congress Control Number: 2024938315

PUBLISHER'S CATALOGING-IN-PUBLICATION DATA

Names: Gates, Margo, author.
Title: Become an aviation pro: flight training, aircraft care & more / by Margo Gates
Other Title: flight training, aircraft care & more
Description: Minneapolis, Minnesota : ABDO Publishing, 2025 | Series: Talent to trade | Includes online resources and index.
Identifiers: ISBN 9781098295004 (lib. bdg.) | ISBN 9798384915058 (ebook)
Subjects: LCSH: Aviation ground crews--Juvenile literature. | Aviation mechanics (Persons)--Juvenile literature. | Aviation communications--Juvenile literature. | Pilots and pilotage--Juvenile literature. | Airplane industry--Juvenile literature. | Jobs--Juvenile literature. | Trades--Juvenile literature.
Classification: DDC 629.132--dc23

CONTENTS

LN-FAV

TALENT TO TRADE

Are you fascinated by how aircraft navigate the sky? Do you love to observe the activity in and around airports? Can you see yourself working with air travelers to ensure their safety? If your answer to any of these questions is yes, you might be suited to a career in aviation.

Becoming an aviation professional includes a lot of training and hard work. It takes a dedication to safety, security, rules, and regulations. But if you have a passion for aviation, you may find that the dedication comes naturally and the hard work is worthwhile.

In this book, you'll learn about the history of aviation and various jobs in the industry. You'll become familiar with some basic tools, skills, and techniques used by aviation pros. You'll find inspiration to begin working toward your own career in aviation. Finally, you'll learn about some of the ways you can turn your talents into a trade.

Bessie Coleman traveled the US performing tricks with her plane, such as flying in loops.

In 1972, a NASA pilot flew an F-8 jet using the fly-by-wire system. This was the first electronic flight control system.

AVIATION THROUGH THE AGES

On December 17, 1903, American brothers Wilbur and Orville Wright went to a beach in North Carolina. There, they launched the first heavier-than-air powered flight. The Wright brothers owe much of this success to Charles Taylor. Taylor was the mechanic who helped design and build their plane's engine. Together, Taylor and the Wright brothers brought about the birth of modern aviation.

In the following decade, national militaries used aircraft in combat during World War I. After the war, American civilian pilots began making aviation history. In 1921, Bessie Coleman became the first Black woman to earn a pilot's license. In 1927, Charles Lindbergh made the first solo, nonstop flight across the Atlantic Ocean. Several years later, Amelia Earhart became the first woman to achieve the same feat.

By 1930, American aerospace company Boeing had established an airline company to transport passengers. Registered nurse Ellen Church convinced Boeing that their flights would benefit from an onboard nurse who could assist passengers and comfort those who were anxious about flying. Boeing hired Church and seven other women to work as some of the country's first flight attendants.

Around the same time, Archie W. League was hired by an airport in St. Louis, Missouri, to help prevent collisions between aircraft. He used a red flag to symbolize "hold" and a checkered flag to symbolize "go." Many consider League to be the first air traffic controller.

Ellen Church was a licensed pilot who wanted to fly planes. But airlines didn't hire female pilots in the 1930s.

The first woman in the US to earn a pilot's license was Harriet Quimby in 1911.

As air traffic in the US increased over the next two decades, the task of keeping aircraft safely separated throughout their flights became more complicated. So airlines worked together to create a more formal air traffic control system. Controllers initially used maps, calipers, and blackboards or paper to track flights. In the 1930s, the British had started developing radar technology. After World War II, air traffic controllers began using radar to track flights.

The 1950s brought what is known as the "golden age of air travel." Boeing's 707 aircraft made air travel faster, safer, and more comfortable. In the 1960s, Boeing developed the 747 "Jumbo Jet," the world's largest passenger aircraft at the time. As airlines fit more passengers onto planes, flying became affordable for more people. Meanwhile, 1971 brought the first automated baggage handling system. This new system used conveyor belts to move passengers' luggage. With the help of ramp agents who loaded and unloaded aircraft and otherwise prepared them for departure or arrival, these systems made air travel more efficient.

Though air travel had become more reliable than ever, it still presented security risks. In September 2001, terrorists hijacked and crashed four flights in an attack against the United States. Afterward, the federal government established the Transportation Security Administration (TSA). The TSA's purpose is to prevent hijackings and other threats. It does this by having Transportation Security Officers (TSOs) conduct screenings of passengers and baggage before flights.

As of 2023, more than 45,000 flights and 2.9 million airline passengers fly each day in the US. And there are more than 19,000 airports and 10 million aviation jobs in the world. In the following pages, you'll learn what it takes to work as a professional in this industry. You may even be inspired to start your journey to becoming an aviation pro right now!

A Lufthansa Boeing 747 is made up of about 6 million parts.

Workers at the Boeing plant in Renton, Washington, can build a Boeing 737 in about nine days.

TOOLS OF THE TRADE

Get familiar with some of the tools aviation professionals use to keep air travel safe, comfortable, and on schedule.

SAFETY & SECURITY

HAND TOOLS

Airplanes and other aircraft are made up of many parts that must be assembled with care. Torque wrenches allow aircraft mechanics to fasten nuts and bolts with a precise amount of force. Needle-nose pliers allow for making small adjustments in tight spaces. Mechanics often organize these and other hand tools in the drawers of mobile tool chests.

VISUAL AIDS

Aircraft mechanics use flashlights to illuminate dark areas. They use mirrors attached to long handles that extend out to view hard-to-reach spaces. To inspect dark and hard to reach areas, mechanics often use a borescope. This device has a long tube that can fit through narrow spaces. At one end of the tube is a camera or other optical system. At the other end is a screen or eyepiece for viewing the footage.

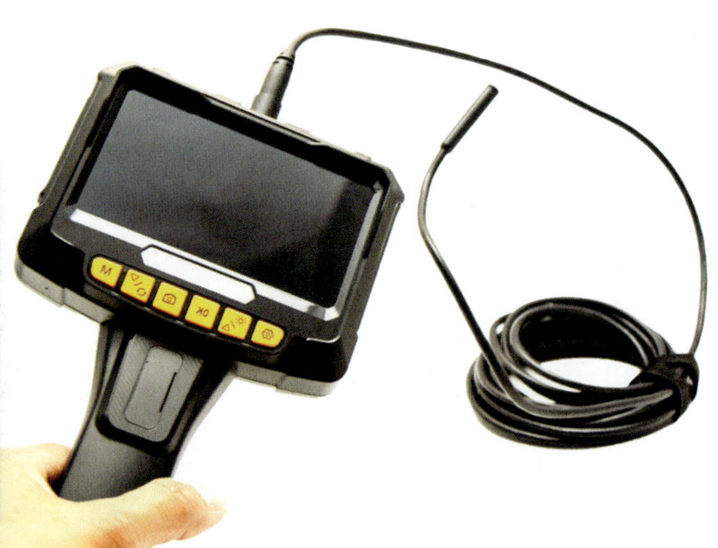

NON-DESTRUCTIVE TESTING

Various testing methods allow mechanics to assess aircraft components without disassembling or damaging them. For example, ultrasonic testing equipment sends sound waves into a material. Mechanics analyze the reflected waves to detect hidden flaws such as cracks or corrosion. Radiographic testing uses X-rays to produce images of internal

structures. This helps mechanics find flaws such as issues with the welding. Magnetic particle testing identifies invisible flaws in magnetic metal materials such as steel. To do so, the material is magnetized and then covered in magnetic particles. The particles cluster around cracks and other defects, making them visible.

ADVANCED IMAGING TECHNOLOGY

At airport security checkpoints, TSOs use advanced imaging technology (AIT). An AIT scanner screens passengers for weapons and explosives that may be hidden under their clothing. Each traveler passes through the AIT scanner, which uses low-energy radiation to scan the body for threats. A TSO agent views a screen that shows any potential threat and its general location on the body.

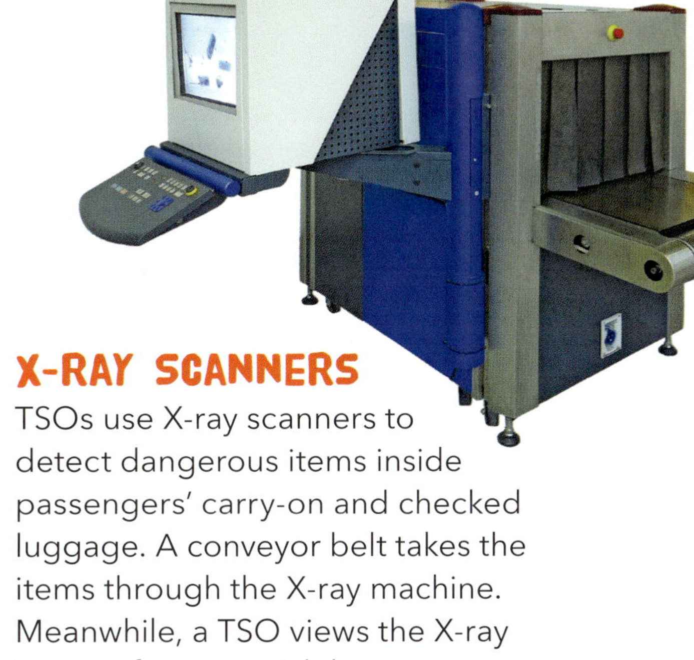

X-RAY SCANNERS

TSOs use X-ray scanners to detect dangerous items inside passengers' carry-on and checked luggage. A conveyor belt takes the items through the X-ray machine. Meanwhile, a TSO views the X-ray images for potential threats.

EXPLOSIVES TRACE DETECTORS

TSOs use explosives trace detectors (ETDs) to screen for small amounts of explosives on passengers or their belongings. First, a TSO wipes a passenger's hands or belongings with a swab. Then, they insert the swab into the ETD, which analyzes the sample in less than a minute.

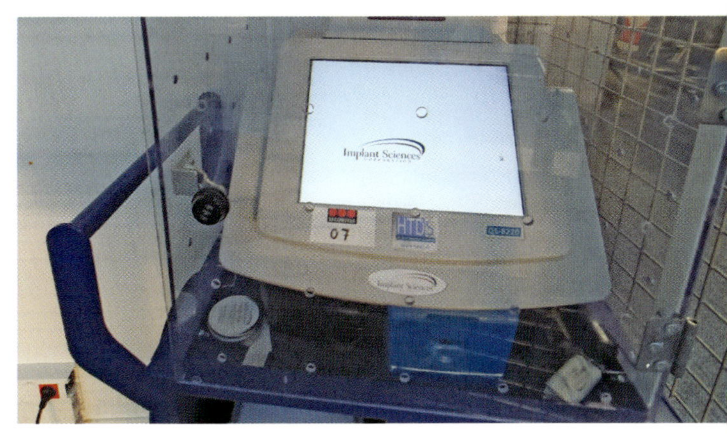

GROUND SUPPORT & CONTROL

MARSHALLING WANDS

Ramp agents use bright wands or paddles to guide pilots as they operate aircraft on the ground. A ramp agent holds and moves a wand in each hand to create signals for the pilot. Every signal has its own meaning, such as turn, proceed, slow down, and stop.

WHEEL CHOCKS

When an aircraft is parked, a ramp agent places wedges called chocks against the wheels. These wedges are usually made of a heavy-duty rubber, metal, or wood. Ramp agents place chocks on both sides of each aircraft wheel. This prevents any accidental movement of the aircraft. The chocks stay in place until the aircraft is ready to depart again.

BELT LOADERS

Belt loaders are vehicles equipped with conveyor belts. A ramp agent positions the vehicle close to the aircraft. Then cargo or passenger luggage are unloaded from the aircraft's cargo compartment and sent down the conveyor belt. Ramp agents then use belt loaders to load the next flight's cargo and luggage onto the aircraft.

DEICERS

In cold weather, snow or ice can build up on an aircraft and create a safety hazard. To prevent this, ramp agents operate deicing trucks or carts. These are vehicles equipped with hoses that spray the plane with a hot fluid to remove existing ice.

Ramp agents may finish the process with anti-icing fluid. This helps prevent further accumulation of ice on the plane's surface.

PUSHBACK TRACTORS

An aircraft cannot back out of the ramp where it is parked on its own. Instead, a small, powerful vehicle called a pushback tractor tows the aircraft to the taxiway. The tractor connects to the landing gear under the nose of the aircraft. A ramp agent operates the tractor to push or pull the aircraft.

RADAR SYSTEMS

Air traffic controllers (ATCs) monitor the airspace with various radar systems. Radar transmitters send radio waves into the atmosphere. The radio waves reflect off flying aircraft and travel back to radar receivers. The radar system can then calculate the approximate location of aircraft within a certain airspace. ATCs also use radar systems to monitor ground traffic on the airfield as well as weather conditions in the surrounding area.

SITUATION DISPLAY

ATCs must be aware of various factors that can affect the flights they are tracking. To do so, they rely on a large computer screen called a situation display.
In addition to showing map information and aircraft positions, this screen can also display weather data, terrain information, areas with traffic restrictions, and more.

COMMUNICATION SYSTEMS

ATCs can speak with pilots in the air by radio frequency. They usually wear headsets to do this easily. As of 2023, the Federal Aviation Administration (FAA) has also been implementing a digital communication system in which ATCs and pilots communicate by text-based messages. This new system is more efficient and less prone to error compared to voice communication.

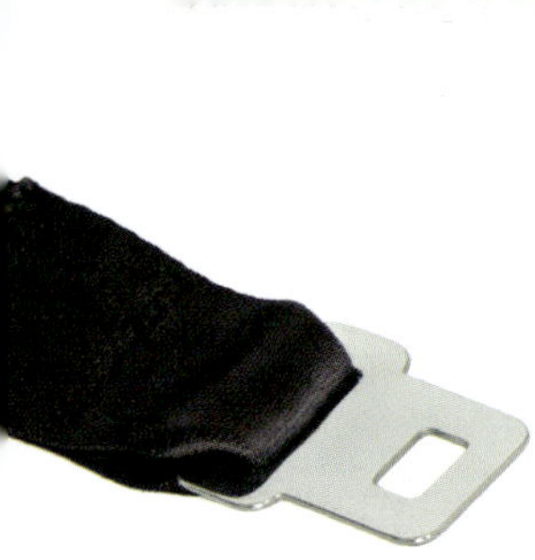

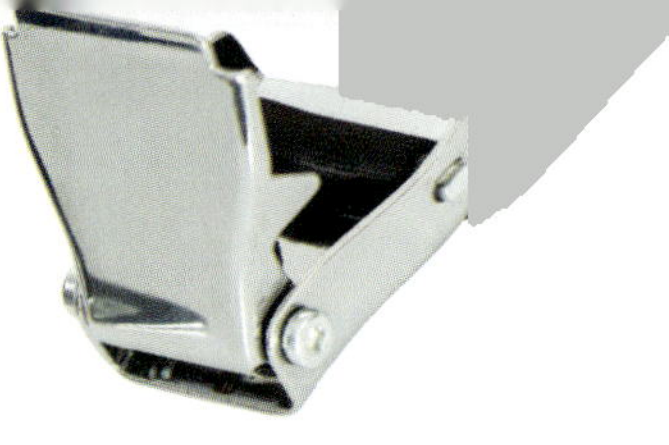

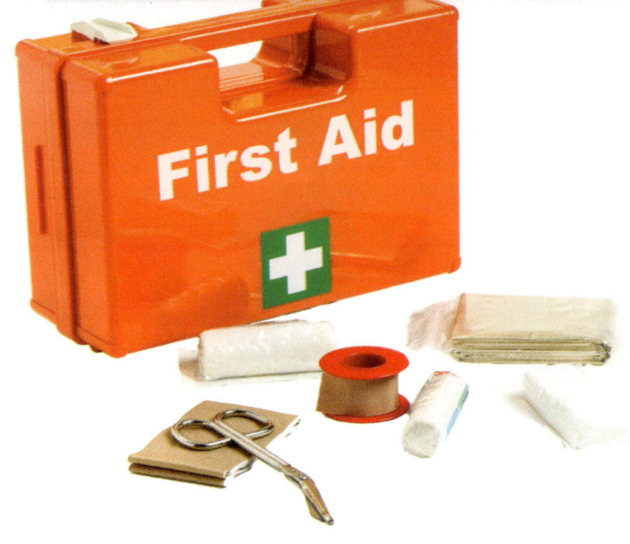

FLIGHT CREW

SAFETY BRIEFING KIT

Before a flight takes off, flight attendants often do a safety demonstration. They show passengers how to secure their seatbelts as well as how to use life vests and oxygen masks in an emergency. They also explain what steps to take in an emergency.

An attendant's safety briefing kit includes these items along with a safety card for passengers to read. Pamphlets with this information are also available in a pocket in front of each seat for passengers to read.

MEDICAL SUPPLIES

Every commercial aircraft must carry medical supplies in case a passenger needs medical attention during a flight. These supplies include syringes, various medicines, a defibrillator, and more. Flight attendants are responsible for making sure an aircraft has all the necessary medical supplies before a flight.

AREA CALL PANEL

Flight attendants must be able to communicate with the pilots, passengers, and each other. On large aircraft, area call panels (ACPs) help attendants quickly see where their attention is needed. An ACP is a series of lights located on the ceiling of the aircraft cabin. Different light colors and flashing patterns have different meanings. These tell attendants if a passenger needs assistance, there is a call from the flight deck, smoke has been detected, and more.

PA & INTERPHONE SYSTEMS

Flight attendants and pilots use a public address, or PA, system to make announcements to all passengers. To speak among each other, the flight crew uses the aircraft's interphone system. For both systems, members of the flight crew speak into a handset or headset.

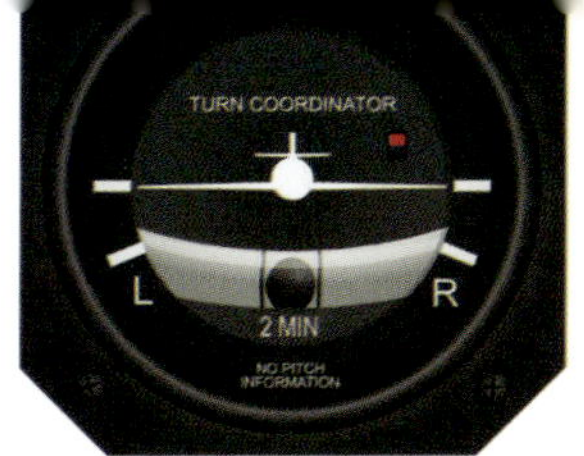

FLIGHT INSTRUMENTS

The instrument panel of a flight deck is full of different types of gauges and dials. But there are a few basic instruments that all aircraft have. The airspeed indicator shows the aircraft's speed. The altimeter shows its height above sea level. The heading and altitude indicators show the aircraft's direction and position in relation to the horizon, respectively. The vertical speed indicator shows the rate of the aircraft's climb or descent. And the turn coordinator shows the rate and direction of a turn. Pilots reference all these instruments to safely fly when visibility is low.

FLIGHT MANAGEMENT SYSTEM

The flight management system (FMS) is a computer and display in the flight deck of an aircraft. The computer uses a variety of data to make calculations that assist the

pilot during flight. For example, the FMS displays an aircraft's flight path, estimated flight time, and fuel requirements. If a pilot must divert from the flight path, the FMS can recalculate flight time and fuel requirements.

AUTOPILOT

An aircraft's FMS works closely with its autopilot system. Autopilot guides the aircraft along its flight path without the pilot's direct assistance. Autopilot can control the majority of a flight. But at any point, the pilot can either adjust the autopilot settings or turn off autopilot and take over manual control of the aircraft.

SPECIAL SKILLS

Explore some of the skills that aviation professionals need to do their jobs.

ATTENTION TO DETAIL

Aircraft mechanics must notice small amounts of wear on aircraft parts. TSOs look out for prohibited items and suspicious activity at airports. ATCs must keep track of all the information on their situation display as they direct flights. And flight attendants must be alert to safety issues on flights. All these tasks require full awareness and attention to detail.

CALM UNDER STRESS

ATCs must react quickly to conditions that can impact the safety of multiple flights. Flight attendants comfort and direct passengers during flight emergencies. Pilots make split-second decisions, such as aborting a landing if the aircraft isn't properly aligned with the runway. In stressful situations like these, aviation professionals must remain calm and decisive.

FLEXIBILITY

Flights are in the air 24 hours a day, 365 days a year. That means most aviation professionals must be willing to work overnight, on weekends, and on holidays. And for long-haul flights, cabin crews may work 14-hour shifts. With schedules like these, workers must be flexible and adaptable.

PROBLEM-SOLVING

Aircraft mechanics use critical thinking and logic to find the source of mechanical issues. ATCs help pilots adjust their flight path or make emergency landings without endangering other aircraft. TSOs and flight attendants must figure out how to handle unruly passengers and potential security risks. Jobs like these require excellent problem-solving skills.

STAMINA

Working in aviation requires both physical and mental stamina. Aircraft mechanics may spend hours holding heavy tools in a cramped space. Ramp agents repeatedly lift heavy luggage and cargo. ATCs must focus on the status of multiple flights at once.

TEAMWORK

Most aviation professionals work closely with others. Ramp agents work together to prepare an aircraft for flight. They also communicate with pilots to guide aircraft to and from the gate. ATCs must give clear instructions to pilots and carefully listen to pilots' responses or requests. Flight crews also work as teams, sharing the many responsibilities of managing a smooth and safe flight.

TECHNICAL SKILLS

Aviation wouldn't be possible without advanced tools and technology. These can include a mechanic's power tools, a ramp agent's belt loader, a pilot's flight instruments, a TSO's X-ray scanner, and more. Aviation pros must have the technical skills and knowledge to operate these devices efficiently.

CAREERS IN AVIATION

There are many types of aviation professionals. They work at airports, on aircraft, and in various other locations. Though their job titles vary, they all work together to make air travel as safe and efficient as possible.

AIRCRAFT MECHANIC

Aircraft mechanics are sometimes known as aviation maintenance technicians. Their job is to maintain, test, and repair aircraft to ensure the safety of the aircraft's passengers and crew. Many aircraft mechanics are employed by airlines, aircraft manufacturers, or the federal government.

ROUTINE MAINTENANCE

Aircraft mechanics perform scheduled maintenance to ensure an aircraft is airworthy, or fit for flight. This maintenance includes inspecting both external and internal parts of aircraft. These include everything from the tires and brakes to the flight controls and electronics. Mechanics often use non-destructive testing tools to identify small amounts of wear. They also clean mechanical parts to prevent corrosion or chemical buildup.

TESTING & REPAIRS

If an aircraft has an electrical or mechanical issue, technicians use non-destructive testing tools and other diagnostic equipment to determine the cause. They may also analyze flight test data to identify performance problems. If an aircraft part is damaged, mechanics use hand tools and power tools to either repair or replace the part.

READING & RECORDKEEPING

Aircraft are complex machines, and each is different from the next. That's why aircraft mechanics must often read instruction manuals. These help mechanics know how to perform maintenance and repair procedures for specific aircraft. In addition to being able to interpret technical language, mechanics must thoroughly document all aircraft maintenance, tests, and repairs. They record details such as what was done, when it was done, and the results. These records help inform those who work on the aircraft in the future.

TRANSPORTATION SECURITY OFFICER

TSOs are employed by the TSA, an agency of the US Department of Homeland Security. A TSO's job is to ensure the safety of travelers. To do this, TSOs screen passengers and baggage before they board aircraft.

CHECKPOINT MANAGEMENT

Most US airports have security checkpoints that travelers must pass through before boarding their flights. TSOs help direct people through these checkpoints. They show travelers where to form lines and inform them about security procedures. TSOs inspect travelers' passports or other forms of identification at the beginning of each checkpoint. To avoid overcrowding and long lines, TSOs give travelers clear directions about where to go, what to do with their personal items, and more.

SCREENING TECHNOLOGY

TSOs are responsible for maintaining and operating various screening devices used to detect potential security threats. All passenger baggage moves on conveyor belts through X-ray machines. These machines

After repairing an aircraft, mechanics need to test their work and any replacement parts. They do this to ensure everything works the way it's supposed to.

TSOs may provide guidance on separating certain carry-on items. This can include separating liquids and electronics into different bins for screening.

Every day, the TSA screens approximately 3.3 million carry-on bags and 1.3 million checked bags!

TSOs may also conduct an extra scan using a handheld metal detector.

provide TSOs with an image of the bags' contents. TSOs also screen passengers to make sure they aren't concealing any weapons or explosives on their bodies. They do this with the help of imaging technology that scans passengers for both metallic and non-metallic threats. While these machines do a lot of the work, TSOs must direct travelers as they operate the machines and constantly monitor the results of the screenings. They also carry out any additional screening procedures if needed.

PHYSICAL SCREENINGS

If the screening technology detects a potential threat, TSOs sometimes conduct physical screenings of baggage and passengers. TSOs are trained to search passenger baggage and belongings with care. If they must search a passenger, they may conduct a pat-down to check for any concealed items beneath the person's clothing. Pat-downs may include inspecting the head, neck, arms, torso, legs, and feet. TSOs may also decide to swab a passenger's hands or belongings to detect traces of explosives.

THREAT RESPONSE

TSOs do not have the authority to make arrests. So, they must communicate any security threats to other officials. This may include airport police, local law enforcement, or the FAA. TSOs might also coordinate with airport or airline staff to address any security issues.

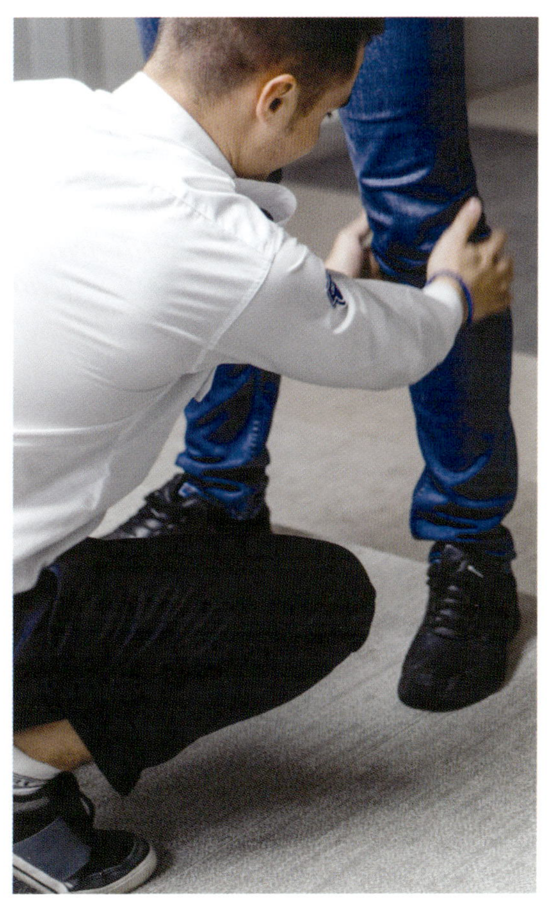

RAMP AGENT

Ramp agents are also sometimes known as ground service agents. They work on the ramp, which is the area outside an airport gate. This is where aircraft park between flights. Ramp agents are often employed by airlines or third-party companies that provide ground handling services. They work to ensure that passengers and cargo move on and off the aircraft in a smooth and timely manner.

AIRCRAFT GUIDANCE

When an aircraft approaches an airport gate, the pilot has a limited view of the ramp. A ramp agent signals to the pilot using marshalling wands or paddles. This helps to guide the pilot as they park the aircraft. When it is time for the aircraft to depart, a ramp agent drives a pushback tractor to tow the aircraft from the ramp to the taxiway.

BOARDING & DEPLANING

Travelers on many commercial airlines board and deplane their aircraft through a passenger boarding bridge. This bridge stretches from the airport gate to the passenger door of the plane. Ramp agents are responsible for setting up this bridge. If the airline doesn't use a boarding bridge, ramp agents set up portable stairs or ramps for passengers to use as they board and deplane.

Ramp agents who guide planes using signals are also known as marshallers.

Sometime passengers may need to walk to the plane. When this happens, ramp agents watch and assist passengers to make sure they board and deplane safely.

A ramp agent usually loads four to eight aircraft each day.

BAGGAGE HANDLING

When an aircraft arrives at an airport, ramp agents unload any cargo and passenger baggage from the plane. They transport everything to a designated location. Then, they load the plane with the cargo and baggage for the next flight. This work involves lifting luggage from baggage carts onto belt loaders. Then, ramp agents manually position the items within the cargo compartment to ensure proper weight distribution.

CLEANING & MAINTENANCE

Between flights, ramp agents clean and restock the aircraft. They empty the lavatory waste tank and refill the water supply. Ramp agents also clean windows, remove snow, and deice the aircraft as needed.

AIR TRAFFIC CONTROLLER

ATCs monitor and direct the movement of aircraft on the ground and in the air. Most ATCs are employed by the FAA. They work at different ground facilities across the country from which they communicate with pilots and other ATCs. Whatever facility they operate in, all ATCs work to minimize air traffic delays and ensure the safety of millions of travelers every day.

TOWER CONTROL

Tower controllers work in an airport control tower. Their job is to direct aircraft and other vehicles on the taxiways and runways. They work to ensure aircraft and vehicles are safely distanced apart. Tower ATCs communicate with pilots of departing and arriving flights. They provide instructions and clearance to take off and land. In the event of a crash, collision, or other emergency, tower controllers alert emergency responders.

APPROACH & DEPARTURE

Once an aircraft is in the air, a Terminal Radar Approach Control (TRACON) facility takes control of the flight. TRACON facilities are located about 20 to 50 miles (32 to 80 km) from airports. ATCs at these facilities monitor traffic within the airspace of one or more airports. Their job is to make sure all aircraft within the airspace are safely distanced from one another and following their designated

Guiding all aircraft safely is the most important part of an ATC's job.

ATCs use radiotelephony when communicating with aircraft. This language uses code words in place of letters and numbers.

An ATC can handle multiple aircraft at the same time.

flight paths. The controllers give arriving flights clearance to enter the airspace. They also hand off control of departing flights to the next ATC.

ROUTE CONTROL

When an aircraft leaves an airport's airspace, they enter the airspace of an Air Route Traffic Control Center (ARTCC). These facilities are located throughout the country. They guide pilots along their routes. For example, an ARTCC controller may advise a pilot to deviate from their flight path to avoid getting too close to another aircraft. Or a controller may suggest a pilot make an altitude adjustment to avoid difficult weather conditions. When an aircraft exits the airspace of one ARTCC, controllers hand it off to the next ARTCC on the flight path.

NATIONWIDE COMMAND

Some ATCs work at the Air Traffic Control Systems Command Center (ATCSCC) in Virginia. There, controllers monitor all traffic within the national airspace. Their job is to coordinate air traffic and minimize delays in the face of unplanned events that affect many flights. Severe weather is a common challenge. The ATCSCC communicates with the National Weather Service, airlines, and ATCs in affected areas to respond to weather-related issues. They may decide to ground, reroute, or delay all flights traveling through the affected region. ATCSCC controllers also help manage planned events, such as rocket launches and presidential flights. These events often require clearing the airspace around the planned event's flight path.

FLIGHT ATTENDANT

Flight attendants work on passenger airplanes to ensure the safety and comfort of travelers during the flight. Most flight attendants are employed by commercial airlines. They may also work on private planes. On most flights, several attendants work as a team to manage a variety of responsibilities.

PREFLIGHT CHECKS

Before a flight, attendants inspect the cabin and lavatories. This ensures everything is clean, no items are missing, and nothing was left behind. They check food and beverage supplies to make sure there is enough for the flight. They also inspect all emergency equipment to confirm that it's functional. As the plane prepares for takeoff, flight attendants walk through the cabin. They check that all passengers have their seatbelts fastened, seats upright, and carry-on items properly stowed.

SAFETY DEMONSTRATION

It's important that all passengers know what to do in case of an emergency. Flight attendants often provide a safety demonstration. They show passengers the location of emergency exits and proper use of safety equipment such as oxygen masks and life vests. Some flights show a video demonstration instead. But flight attendants are always available to answer questions about emergency procedures. They also communicate with any passengers sitting in emergency exit rows to confirm that they are willing and able to assist in an emergency.

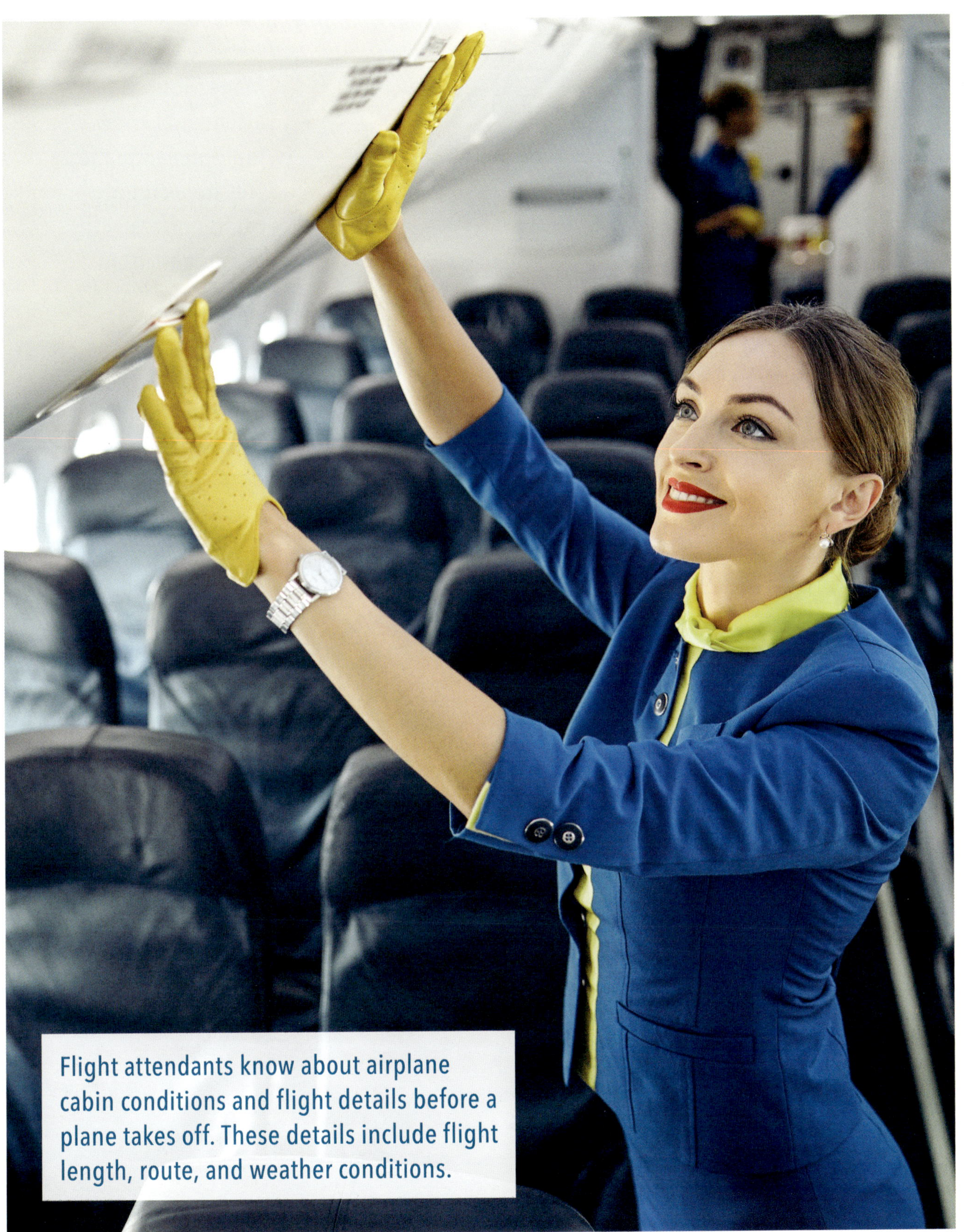

Flight attendants know about airplane cabin conditions and flight details before a plane takes off. These details include flight length, route, and weather conditions.

Many flight attendants know multiple languages. This helps them communicate with passengers from around the world.

Flight attendants assess passengers as they welcome them onto a plane. This helps them determine if passengers may be a safety risk, helpful in an emergency, and more.

CUSTOMER SERVICE

A big part of a flight attendant's job is making sure the passenger experience is as comfortable and positive as possible. Flight attendants greet travelers as they board the aircraft. They help passengers find their seats and stow their luggage. They may hand out headphones, blankets, and other items to enhance the flight experience. Attendants serve snacks, beverages, and sometimes full meals during the flight. They are also always available to answer questions and kindly reassure anxious passengers.

INCIDENT RESPONSE

While flight attendants are busy providing customer service, they stay alert for possible issues. They are prepared to respond if a problem arises. Flight attendants monitor the cabin for signs of disruption, medical issues, and security threats. They are trained to administer basic first aid, CPR, and other medical attention. They are also able to extinguish fires and restrain passengers who are putting others in danger. And they direct passengers in emergency situations.

PILOT

Pilots operate and navigate aircraft. Some pilots fly in the military. Others fly private planes for companies or individuals. But most US pilots are employed by commercial airlines to transport passengers or cargo. Airline pilots typically fly in teams of two. They share the many duties involved in safely navigating an aircraft through every stage of flight.

PREFLIGHT

Before a flight, pilots review the flight plan. The flight plan includes the route an aircraft will take to its destination. It also includes considerations such as airspace restrictions, weather forecasts, and more. Pilots may review technical data and maintenance records for the aircraft. They inspect the aircraft and its various systems to confirm it is airworthy.

TAKEOFF & CLIMB

When the aircraft is ready to depart, ramp agents tow it from the airport gate to the taxiway. Pilots then communicate with tower ATCs to receive clearance for takeoff on a designated runway. During takeoff, pilots focus on maintaining the aircraft's stability. They must react quickly to disruptions. For example, wind gusts can suddenly change the angle of the aircraft's nose or cause the aircraft to drift sideways. After takeoff, pilots increase the aircraft's speed and altitude to climb to cruising altitude.

Pilots review a list of all required preflight checks before every flight.

Takeoff and landing can be the hardest part of a pilot's job. Pilots need to coordinate with other pilots, ATCs, and others to safely navigate the plane.

Pilots need to have good vision and cannot be color-blind.

CRUISE

Cruising altitude is the height that an aircraft stays at for most of the flight. Pilots often activate the aircraft's autopilot during this flight stage. Even then, pilots monitor engine performance, fuel consumption, and other aircraft systems. They communicate with ATC facilities along their route. They are also prepared to follow ATC guidance if the aircraft's flight path needs to be adjusted. And pilots stay alert and are ready to respond to unexpected situations. This can include weather events, mechanical issues, and passenger emergencies.

DESCEND & LAND

When a flight is nearing its destination, the pilots prepare the aircraft for landing. This process includes decreasing altitude and speed and lowering the aircraft's landing gear. At the same time, pilots continue communicating with ATCs for landing clearance and instructions. Just before touchdown, pilots use a technique called the flare. This means they raise the nose of the plane. This brings the plane parallel to the ground, allowing for a smooth landing. Pilots typically land planes manually. But if visibility is poor due to weather conditions, pilots may use the aircraft's autopilot to help land the plane.

CREATE YOUR VISION

It's time to get creative! Think about your hobbies and interests that relate to aviation. Create a vision board that reflects these and whatever else inspires you. Let it motivate you to turn your talents into your trade!

Put your vision board where you'll see it on a regular basis, such as in your locker or next to your bed.

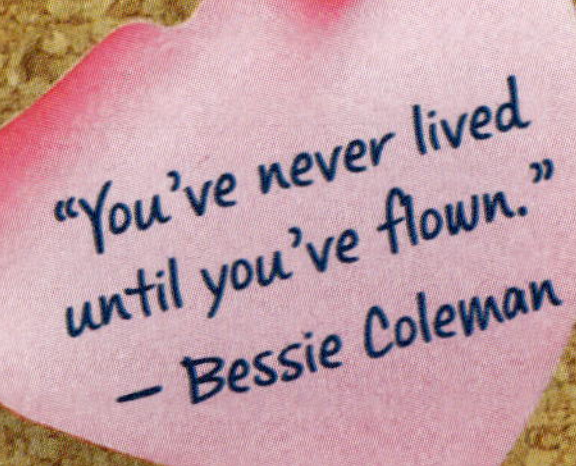

Amelia Earhart
Display magazine pages, quotes, and photos that reflect what you love about aviation.
"The most effective way to do it is to do it."
— Amelia Earhart

EXPLORE YOUR ELECTIVES

You've got the vision. Now get in the classroom! Choose high school and postsecondary electives that will give you knowledge relevant to your goal.

Take a class in electronics or auto mechanics if you think you'd like to repair or operate aircraft.

If you'd like to work in airport security, take a psychology or sociology course to better understand human behavior.

Learn a foreign language or two if you plan to serve travelers from around the world as a flight attendant.

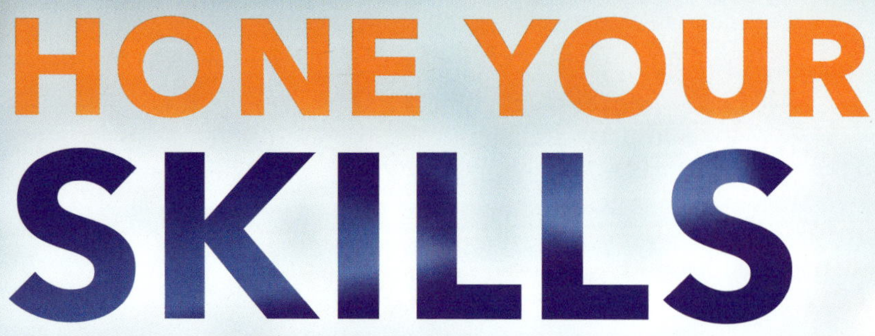

HONE YOUR SKILLS

Start taking steps to develop valuable technical and transferable skills that would be valuable in any future job. Transferable skills include communication, leadership, and more.

Develop your ability to communicate and collaborate through hobbies, like playing in a band or joining a team sport.

Practice multitasking and time management by cooking a meal for your family or babysitting.

Practice flying by using a flight simulator video game such as Microsoft Flight Simulator.

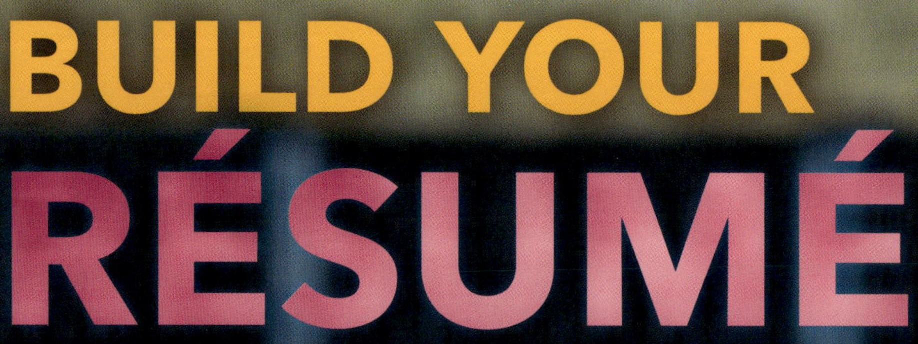

BUILD YOUR RÉSUMÉ

Find a part-time job or volunteer opportunity that gives you experience relevant to your future role. Include these positions and your responsibilities within them on your résumé.

Do you want to be a flight attendant? Work at a restaurant, hotel, or community food pantry where you interact with and serve customers.

Do you want to be a ramp agent? Get experience doing physical labor and operating small vehicles by doing park maintenance or working for a moving company.

LIFEGUARD
Do you want to be a TSO? Get experience in public safety by working as a crowd manager, lifeguard, or park patrol.

BUILD YOUR OWN PLANE

Explore the joys of flight by making your own model plane. When you're done, throw it in the air and watch it fly!

Tip! Experiment with different lengths of wings and thicknesses of body shape. How can you improve the design and make it your own?

SUPPLIES

- 20 by 30 inch (50.8 by 76.2 cm) foam board
- pencil
- ruler
- scissors
- hot glue gun
- 3 sheets of 9 by 12 inch (22.9 by 30.5 cm) craft foam
- paint and paint brush (optional)

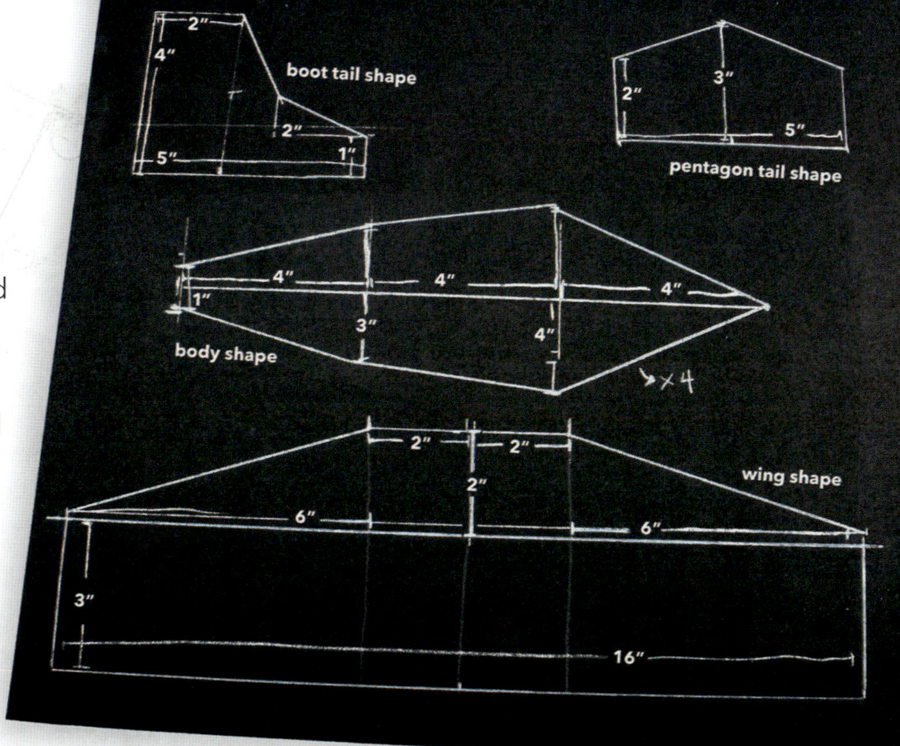

STEPS

1 Following the diagram on the right, measure and cut the plane's wing, body, boot tail, and pentagon tail shapes out of the foam board.

2 Use the body shape to trace and cut four more body shapes out of the foam board.

3 Lay a body shape on a flat surface. Center the wing shape onto the body shape so the long sides are perpendicular to the body shape. Make sure the straight side is facing the body shape's blunt end. Glue the two shapes together.

4 Measure and cut a 1 inch (2.5 cm) long notch in the center of the body shape's blunt end. Make the notch as wide as the thickness of the foam board.

5 Repeat step 4 to cut a notch in the center of the short side of the boot tail shape.

6 Repeat step 4 to cut a notch on the opposite side of the boot tail shape so that it lines up with the first notch.

7 Repeat step 4 to cut a notch in the pointed end of the pentagon tail shape.

8 Slide the two tail shapes together using the notches you made from steps 6 and 7.

9 Use a body shape to trace and cut six body shapes out of the craft foam sheets. Trim down the sides near the pointed end of each shape so that when they are stacked, each shape's pointed end is a little shorter than the one below it. Trim and place three foam board body shapes in between the craft foam body shapes. Keep one of the foam board body shapes on the very bottom.

10 Repeat step 4 to cut 2 inch (5.1 cm) long notches in each body shape's blunt end. Make sure all the notches line up when the shapes are stacked.

11 Layer and glue the body shapes on top of the stacked body and wing piece from largest to smallest, lining up the notched ends.

12 Trim down the front and back sides of the last foam board body shape so it fits on top of the stacked body and wing piece. Glue it down.

13 Slide the connected tail shapes onto the stacked body and wing piece using the notches.

14 Trim any rough edges. If you used colored foam board, paint the foam edges with matching colored paint.

BECOMING AN AVIATION PRO

TRAINING

Are you ready for your formal training to be an aviation professional? Some employers may provide training for certain aviation jobs. For example, ramp agents and flight attendants are usually trained by the airline or other company that hires them. Most other aviation professionals require specialized training.

TSOs and ATCs go to specialized schools to receive the education they need for their jobs. After TSOs are hired, they are trained at a TSA Academy. And ATCs attend the FAA Academy before being placed at an airport.

Aircraft mechanics can attend a technical school or receive on-the-job training. This prepares them for FAA certification exams. These exams include written tests, oral interviews, and practical demonstrations.

Pilots also undergo extensive training before they can work for an airline. The rules and certification requirements depend on the type of aircraft a pilot wants to fly and what kind of flying they do. For example, some requirements for commercial pilots flying for major airlines include flight school, at least 1,500 hours of total flight time, and certification exams.

PRE-EMPLOYMENT SCREENING

Aviation professionals play a major role in traveler safety. That's why aviation employers screen prospective employees to ensure they are mentally and physically fit for the job. One pre-employment screening is a background check. This gives employers information about a person's criminal history, driving records, employment history, and more. Other screenings include aptitude tests, medical evaluations, and psychological assessments.

CAREER PROGRESSION

Many aviation professionals receive certifications that they must maintain. They do this through continued training or regular evaluations. This keeps workers up to date on new aircraft, screening technology, safety standards, and more. As workers gain more experience, they may gain access to certain benefits. For example, those with more seniority often have more control over their schedules. They may also receive more vacation days or priority pick in taking holidays off.

Some ATCs and pilots train with simulation tools and equipment.

MEET SOME PROS: US AIRWAYS FLIGHT 1549 CREW

In January 2009, US Airways Flight 1549 had just taken off from a New York City airport when it ran into a flock of geese. The birds knocked out both engines, causing the plane to lose power. Pilot Chesley Sullenberger III made a quick decision to land the plane in the Hudson River. Once Sullenberger crash-landed the plane on the water, the flight attendants safely evacuated all 150 passengers onto rescue boats. The event is remembered as the "Miracle on the Hudson."

The Flight 1549 crew (*from left to right*): Captain Chesley Sullenberger III; flight attendants Doreen Welsh, Sheila Dail, and Donna Dent; and first officer Jeffrey Skiles

TRADES AT WORK

EARNING POTENTIAL

The US Bureau of Labor Statistics provides estimated wage ranges for most workers in any given job category. The ranges below are from May 2023. These estimates provide a sense of what you could expect to earn. However, actual salaries can vary greatly depending on where you work, your experience, and any specialized skills you have.

GROW YOUR POTENTIAL

Whatever salary you start at, there are various ways to grow your earning potential throughout your career. Here are a few ways you can boost your income while continuing to do what you love.

Put in the time. Workers who stay with the same company over time can be eligible for promotions. These often come with an increase in pay. For example, flight attendants can gain enough work experience to become senior cabin crew members. Ramp agents and ATCs can be promoted to supervising or management roles.

Keep learning. Some aviation professionals can work to obtain additional certifications or specializations that qualify them for pay increases. For example,

JOB CATEGORY	ANNUAL SALARY
Aircraft Mechanics and Service Technicians	$59,000-$88,000
Transportation Security Screeners	$45,000-$56,000
Aircraft Cargo Handling Supervisors	$50,000-$76,000
Air Traffic Controllers	$97,000-$177,000
Flight Attendants	$50,000-$87,000
Airline Pilots, Copilots, and Flight Engineers	$143,000-$239,000

an aircraft mechanic might work to become an Airframe and Powerplant mechanic. These mechanics specialize in both the airframe and engine of aircraft. Pilots can also earn more as they obtain additional certificates. If you are a pilot, you might transition from a private pilot to a commercial pilot to an airline transport pilot.

Look beyond your current role. A TSO might pursue a leadership role within the TSA. A ramp agent could go on to work as an airport executive. A flight attendant could freelance for private clients. If you get creative, you may discover multiple paths that branch from the one you're currently on.

FINANCIAL SMARTS

However you're making money, it's important to manage your finances wisely.

If you have an employer, you will receive a regular paycheck from them. This income will be your wages minus taxes. If your employer offers health insurance, retirement savings, or any other benefits, those will also be deducted from your take-home pay. Financial experts recommend you put about 20 percent of each paycheck into savings and try to keep an emergency fund with three to six months' worth of living expenses.

If you are self-employed, you will receive payments directly from your various clients. You'll need to track this income along with your business expenses, such as travel costs and supplies. Self-employed individuals must also pay their own taxes, generally four times a year, since they don't have an employer withholding taxes from each paycheck. Business owners use the remaining profits to pay themselves as well as fund savings accounts—for both themselves and the business!

DO WHAT YOU LOVE!

Being an aviation professional requires teamwork, flexibility, problem-solving, and more. Finding success in aviation work can take years of training. It also takes a commitment to keep learning and growing your skills. Many aviation pros find the time and effort is worth the rewards of keeping air travel smooth, safe, and comfortable.

Maybe your goal is to work in airport security. Maybe you have your sights set on aircraft maintenance or ground support. Or perhaps you want to take to the skies as a member of a flight crew. Or you dream of flying an aircraft and transporting passengers around the world. As long as you do what you love, you'll love what you do.

GLOSSARY

airframe–the parts that create an aircraft's structure.

analyze–to examine something to find out what it is or what makes it work.

assess–to determine the importance, value, or condition of something. An assessment is the process or result of assessing something.

caliper–a tool used to measure the diameter or distance between surfaces.

clearance–the permission given to an aircraft to move forward or continue on its course.

conveyor belt–a mechanical device such as a revolving belt that carries something from one place to another.

deplane–to leave a plane.

diagnostic–used in the study of something to find a problem.

disruption–the act of causing a disturbance.

divert–to change from one course to a different one.

efficient–able to produce a desired result, especially without wasting time or energy. Efficiently means to do a task in a way that does not waste time or energy.

elective–a class that counts towards graduation but is not required.

flight deck–the area where a pilot sits and navigates an aircraft.

gauge–a measuring device.

hijack–to take over or the act of taking over by threatening violence.

interphone–a telephone system used in a small area such as an airplane, ship, or office.

lavatory–a bathroom.

monitor–to watch, keep track of, or oversee.

potential–capable of being or becoming.

priority–the condition of coming before others, as in order or importance.

specialize—to develop expertise in a certain area, called a specialty. Specialized means suited to a particular purpose or occupation.

stamina—the power to endure fatigue, disease, or hardship.

torque—a force that causes turning or twisting.

ultrasonic—a frequency unable to be heard by the human ear.

World War I—from 1914 to 1918, fought in Europe. Great Britain, France, Russia, the United States, and their allies were on one side. Germany, Austria-Hungary, and their allies were on the other side.

World War II—from 1939 to 1945, fought in Europe, Asia, and Africa. Great Britain, France, the United States, the Soviet Union, and their allies were on one side. Germany, Italy, Japan, and their allies were on the other side.

ONLINE RESOURCES

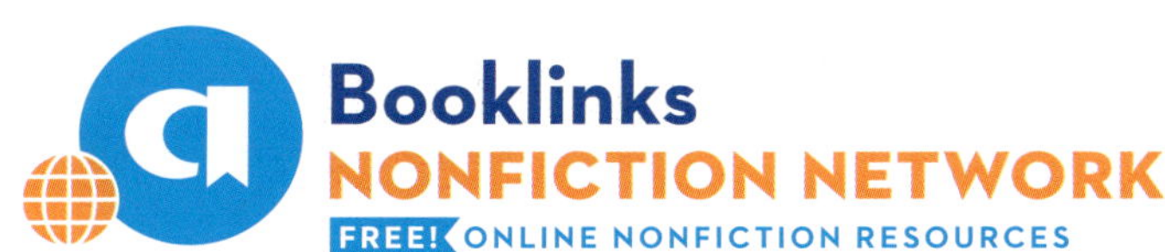

To learn more about trades in aviation, please visit **abdobooklinks.com** or scan this QR code. These links are routinely monitored and updated to provide the most current information available.

INDEX